HOW TO MAKE JEWELRY WITH TATTY DEVINE

HOW TO MAKE JEWELRY WITH TATTY DEVINE

Harriet Vine and Rosie Wolfenden

A PERIGEE BOOK

A PERIGEE BOOK
Published by the Penguin Group
Penguin Group (USA) Inc.
375 Hudson Street, New York, New York 10014, USA

Penguin Group (Canada), 90 Eglinton Avenue East, Suite 700, Toronto, Ontario M4P 2Y3, Canada
(a division of Pearson Penguin Canada Inc.) · Penguin Books Ltd., 80 Strand, London WC2R 0RL,
England · Penguin Ireland, 25 St. Stephen's Green, Dublin 2, Ireland (a division of Penguin
Books Ltd.) · Penguin Group (Australia), 707 Collins Street, Melbourne, Victoria 3008, Australia
(a division of Pearson Australia Group Pty Ltd.) · Penguin Books India Pvt. Ltd., 11 Community
Centre, Panchsheel Park, New Delhi—110 017, India · Penguin Group (NZ), 67 Apollo Drive,
Rosedale, Auckland 0632, New Zealand (a division of Pearson New Zealand Ltd.) · Penguin Books
(South Africa), Rosebank Office Park, 181 Jan Smuts Avenue, Parktown North 2193, South Africa ·
Penguin China, B7 Jiaming Center, 27 East Third Ring Road North, Chaoyang District,
Beijing 100020, China

Penguin Books Ltd., Registered Offices: 80 Strand, London WC2R 0RL, England

While the author has made every effort to provide accurate telephone numbers,
Internet addresses, and other contact information at the time of publication, neither
the publisher nor the author assumes any responsibility for errors, or for changes that
occur after publication. Further, the publisher does not have any control over and does
not assume any responsibility for author or third-party websites or their content.

HOW TO MAKE JEWELRY WITH TATTY DEVINE

First American edition: February 2013
Originally published in Great Britain by Virgin Books in 2011.

ISBN: 978-0-399-16171-1

PRINTED IN THE UNITED STATES OF AMERICA

10   9   8   7   6   5   4   3   2   1

Most Perigee books are available at special quantity discounts for
bulk purchases for sales promotions, premiums, fund-raising, or educational use.
Special books, or book excerpts, can also be created to fit specific needs. For details, write:
Special Markets, Penguin Group (USA) Inc., 375 Hudson Street, New York, New York 10014.

Acknowledgments

Nina Ziegler for designing this book and getting it so right.

Eithne Farry for her way with words.

John William for understanding what goes on in our minds.

Dominic Mifsud for being such a patient photographer.

Saga Sig for taking such perfect pictures of people.

Hannah Knowles, our editor, and everyone at Virgin Books and Ebury Publishing.

To all our models: Becki, Irene, Amelie, Theresa, Ella, Bridie and Sami Knight, hairdresser extraordinaire.

And to everyone who has ever helped, inspired and been part of the adventure so far: Ann and Roger Vine, John and Rosalind Wolfenden, Freda Smith, Joan Wolfenden, Ben Vine, Bebe Higgins, Netia Costa, Rebecca Andreae, William Wolfenden, Harry and Ned, Jack and Tom, Dan Higgins and Tony Collins.

All of Team Tatty, past present and future! You're much loved and appreciated. In no particular order: Thelma and Paul, Mark Pawson, Rachael Matthews, Louise Harries, Nervous Stephen, Joe Egg, Herve and Paul, Nicky Abrahams, Elvina Flower, Mikey, Nick Philips, Mike and Jen, Ilona, Melissa, Rebecca and Amber, Heather, Steph, Nick Pankhurst, Liela and Luke, Fancy Smith, Dino, Matt Dawson, Susanna Edwards, Zeel, Rob Ryan, Hayley, Dan Holiday, *Eel* zine, Adam Wright, Amaia, Amelia, Rocky, Bev, Mimi, Little Miss Lucifer, Jo and Simon, Austin and Clare, Rachel, Sophie and Sabrina, Cleo Ferin, Alex Barrows and the Severed Limb, Rae Jones, Anna Marie, Sandy Waibl, Anat and Jet, Jacey, Antoni and Alison, Mark and Wak, Camera Obscura, Peaches, Chicks on Speed, Gilbert and George, Electrocute, Cobra Killer, Duke Spirit, Lulu Kennedy, Michael from Blow, Basso and Brooke, Barry Newman, Tai Shani, Oh My God! I Miss You, Duke of Uke, Barbara Ryan, Angharad Lewis, Robots in Disguise, Charlie le Mindu, Pil and Galia, Paul Michael, Minna Parika, Rosie Cooper, Ruth Hiki, Georgina Starr and Paul Noble, Harry Woodrow, Susanna Heron, Clyde Hopkins, Roger Ackling, Tara D'Cruz-Noble, Calvin Holbrook, Mary Hanson, Claire Catterall, Design Beckons, Bobby McGees, Skinny Girl Diet, Suburban Mousewife, Mr. Ministeck, Mrs. Jones, Tobin Ireland, Bob and Sally, Barry Stillwell, Verena Paloma Jabs, Ashish, Chrome Hoof, Tokyo Dragons, John Brown and Fiona, Jamie Beeden, Nils, StereoTotal, Rubbishmen, Hilary at the French House, Rollergirls, Supermarket Sarah, Miss High Leg Kick and Richard Hutt, Bishi, Pippa Brooks, Victoria Woodcock, Emily Beaver, Blue Firth, Jamie J, Jeremy Deller, Princess Julia, Scottee, Philip Gwyn Jones, Ryan Styles, Jamie, Rory, Lucy, Philip Normal, Squat, Delia Sparrow, The Actionettes, Richard Roberts and Rosemary, Tessa Clist, Emily Maben, Russel Martin, Lisa Jones, Kim Jenkins, Will Fowler, Charlie Phillips, Fiona from Banchory, Belle and Sebastian, and every other band that has created the soundtrack to Tatty Devine.

Intro

It all started
with a white
leather wrist
cuff, made from
a snippet of an
old belt and held
together by a hair
clip…

Even before we met each other at art school, we'd always made things. We were the sort of girls who painted the scenery for school plays or backdrops for local bands, made our own hair scrunchies, and transformed rocks into ladybugs and bumblebees with enamel paint and sold them as doorstops in the summer holidays. At college we cut up our jeans and made them into skirts, fringed our T-shirts, made clothes from old patterns salvaged from thrift stores and pretty much customized everything we went out in. And we needed a lot of looks for a lot of going out. We'd go and see bands and head out dancing and whatever we wore or made got ruined from high kicking on the bar, or rolling around on the floor of gig venues.

We knew we wanted to keep on making stuff for a living, but we weren't exactly sure what—or how to go about it.

A chance find of a mountain of leather sample books abandoned outside an upmarket furniture shop set us on the path that led to becoming Tatty Devine. Harriet found them on her way back from the pub, carted them home in the dead of night and shoved them under her bed, where they languished for months. She had been wearing a leather cuff, sliced off a white lattice-work belt and held together with a hair clip, that had been getting lots of compliments. So, armed with craft knives and a lot of enthusiasm, we set about making some similar cuffs to sell. We cut up the sample books—they were a treasure trove of colored leather, suede, snakeskin and ostrich skin in every shade of the rainbow—and abandoned the hair clip for a more secure fastening invented by Harriet's dad, Roger. And then we waited in the early hours to get a stall in a flea market. On our first day out at Camden Market, a boy bought a cuff to put in a time capsule. It seemed like a lucky sign.

It was cold and damp at our stall—we had to make cardboard insoles for our shoes to keep our feet warm, and we dreamt of hot baths and glasses of whisky as the wind whistled around our ears—but mostly we loved it. It was so exciting; you never knew who was going to walk up to the stall—stylists, boutique owners or friends, and people who would become friends and collaborators. We loved the camaraderie. At the end of the day we would make deals with other stallholders and get some brilliant stuff. Starting the business this way gave us the freedom to not get real jobs and remain outside the mainstream.

We learned to look at things in a different way. To tilt our heads to the side and see what happened.

We were hooked and wanted to make more and more. We made one-off designs from bits and pieces we found in thrift stores, yard sales and markets. We transformed guitar picks, cake decorations, darts and chess pieces into earrings and charm bracelets, necklaces and hair bobbles. The Internet didn't really exist then (can you believe that?), so we sourced everything locally, using stuff that we found in shops or Dumpsters; instead of using Craigslist or eBay, we took to the pavements, or to stationery shops and DIY emporiums. We were forced to be inventive. We popped our first collection in pink and white striped paper bags like old-fashioned pick'n'mix, and when we got our first fax machine (the height of technology at the time!) we felt-tipped the new number onto the bosoms of our T-shirts, took pictures, made finger puppets from the images and sent

Rosie as a finger puppet. We made a load of them, all with different hairstyles.

A leftover token from a favorite hangout.

them out as our calling cards. There was no grand plan: it was all naïve, instinctive and, above all, fun.

After getting a surprise order from a famous shop, we spent hot summer days gluing crystals onto belts, as forty tortoises mistook our varnished nails for cherry tomatoes in Rosie's east London garden. Another order was assembled in the front room, with our friends as a mini-production line, sewing big fake jewels onto belts and trying not to prick their fingers and bleed onto the white leather. We'd go to bed surrounded by the smell of contact adhesive and suede, and wake up bursting with ideas, learning new techniques and tricks as we went along.

We quickly realized that with some basic skills and a huge amount of imagination anyone can make original and stylish jewelry. As the years have gone by, we've moved from the huddle of our bedrooms and chilly market stalls to setting up a proper studio space and opening two shops. But we still feel exactly the way we did at the beginning. Nothing beats the amazing feeling of making something and heading out on the town with a brooch or a lovely new necklace inspired by a macramé owl discovered at a yard sale, or simply wearing a little of what you fancy, strung together and made into something unique.

And that's what this book is all about. It's about understanding some very basic jewelry-making techniques, and then letting your imagination run wild. There's not going to be anything here that's too tricky to understand, and it won't cost the earth in equipment and supplies. We'll explain how to make necklaces, leather cuffs, tape-measure rosettes and a whole jewelry box full of other accessories, using recycled and upcycled bits and bobs. We'll let you know what inspires us, share some Tatty Devine secrets, and give you the confidence to get making.

No training or big costs involved. Just good friends and a good eye.

Buttons are always brilliant. Our friend Marc Pawson is the King!

A lovely addition to our tin collection, the graphics are really beautiful.

Tools and Findings

Although it's tempting to head out and buy loads of rainbow-colored pliers, glue guns, drills and billions of crystals, and then stack them away in expensive plastic containers, it's nicer to make your own crafty corner with things you love.

When we started we stored our bits and pieces in lovely old cigar boxes collected by Rosie, first-aid tins and odd little boxes that we salvaged from thrift stores. It was a treat to get them out when we were looking for a button or bead. The shelves in our Brick Lane studio were lined with recycled glass jars: we ate a lot of gherkins and some very choice pickles, and then we screwed the jars to the undersides of our shelves by their lids (we washed the jars out first). That way we could use the base of the shelves for storing even more jars and bits and bobs. Space has always been at a premium for us, as we are terrific hoarders.

HOW TO MAKE GENIUS STORAGE

Pimp Your Shelf

You'll need:

Empty jars

Pencil

Scrap wood

Drill

2 mm drill bit

Phillips screwdriver bit

2 screws per jar
(The screws must be shorter than the depth of the shelves)

Cup hooks

Eat the contents of the jars, and then wash them out.

Unscrew the jar lids. Think about where you'd like them to go, and then draw around the lids on the underside of the shelves, using the pencil. Leave enough space between the jars so you can get your hand in to unscrew them.

On the inside of the jar lid, make two marks about 3 cm apart in the center of the lid.

Lay the lid on a bit of scrap wood and drill two holes right where your pencil marks are, using the 2 mm drill bit.

Hold the lid up to the circle you've drawn on the underside of the shelf, and poke the pencil through the holes you've just drilled. These dots are where the screws are going to go.

Now drill a tiny hole onto the pencil dots. Don't drill right through the shelf!

Swap the drill bit for a Phillips screwdriver bit and grab the screws. Hold the lid up to the penciled circle, and push the screws into the tiny holes; give them a little twist so that they don't drop out when you're reaching for the drill.

Using the Phillips screwdriver bit, whoosh in the two screws. You need to have two screws or the jars will just spin round and round like a record and never undo!

Fill up the jars with all your bits and bobs and cool stuff and twist on to the lids.

Screwing cup hooks in between the jars is great too; you can hang work-in-progress necklaces on them, lengths of chain and dangly earrings, rulers, tape measures and key rings. They're also really handy if you need something to hook onto when you're making a long braid or embarking on a piece of macramé.

TOOLS

All the equipment you'll need to get started:

| 2 pairs of flat-nose pliers | Round-nose pliers | Wire cutters | A pair of hefty pliers | Handheld hole punch |

2 pairs of flat-nose pliers:
These are essential. You'll need them for opening jump rings (see page 24) and other bits of jewelry construction. Treat yourself, as these are the things that you'll use the most. But make sure you get smooth ones, not ones with ridges or teeth, as they mark the metal.

Round-nose pliers:
These are handy for curling wire. You can get ones with built-in wire cutters, which we like.

Wire cutters:
For snipping heavy wire and chain. You could use an old pair of scissors, but don't use your best pair as cutting wire will wreck the blades.

A pair of hefty pliers:
For tougher jobs. You can get great ones at yard sales.

Handheld hole punch:
The one on your office desk isn't going to be much help. Instead invest in a handheld punch with a variety of hole sizes.

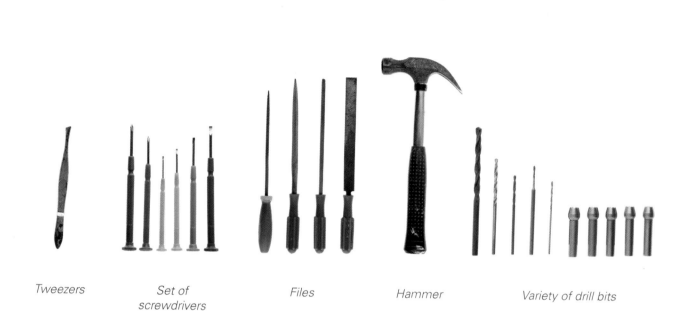

Tweezers

Set of screwdrivers

Files

Hammer

Variety of drill bits

Tweezers:
For fiddly moments with tiny jump rings, fine chain or small crystals.

Set of screwdrivers:
For the doing and undoing of screws.

Files:
A small set of files come into their own for smoothing sharp bits or jagged edges.

Hammer:
For bashing things.

Hand drill or pendant drill:
Very useful, but they can be expensive. Borrow one from a DIY fiend, or go halves with a friend or partner in crime.

Variety of drill bits:
Invest in a selection of small drill bits: 0.8, 1.2, 1.8, 2, 2.5 and 3 mm are the sizes to go for.

Collets:
These hold tiny drill bits in place snugly in the drill.

| Utility knife/ craft knife/scalpel | Hacksaw | Needlework scissors | Pinking shears | Scribe and bradawl | Soft brush | Paintbrushes |

Utility knife/craft knife/ scalpel:
All of these cut with a lovely clean line. Remember to stock up on spare super-sharp blades.

Hacksaw:
This little saw will make light work of stuff that defeats the wire cutters.

Scissors:
You really need a few pairs, such as paper scissors, fabric scissors, pinking shears, an all-around pair (for rough-and-ready jobs) and an elegant pair of needlework scissors for intricate jobs. Our favorites are bird shaped.

Scribe and bradawl:
Handy for marking, scoring and scuffing the surfaces of things that are going to be glued. And for bashing a pilot hole.

Soft brush:
Lovely for brushing away dust and debris and for the final bit of sprucing up on a project.

Paintbrushes:
A selection is a good thing. Use them for painting, staining, gluing and varnishing. Always clean out your brushes properly.

Thimble | Knitting needles | Pins | Tape measure | 2-part epoxy glue | Superglue | Contact adhesive | Glue gun

Thimble:
Sewing leather and heavy fabric can be tough, so a thimble will protect your fingers.

Knitting needles:
A small knitting needle is great if you need to poke something, or if you want to get busy with the glue but your object is small and you're all fingers and thumbs.

Pins:
Handy for poking and pinning.

Tape measure:
For measuring longer things like ribbons and chains.

Glue:
Two-part epoxy resin glue, superglue, contact adhesive and a hot glue gun.

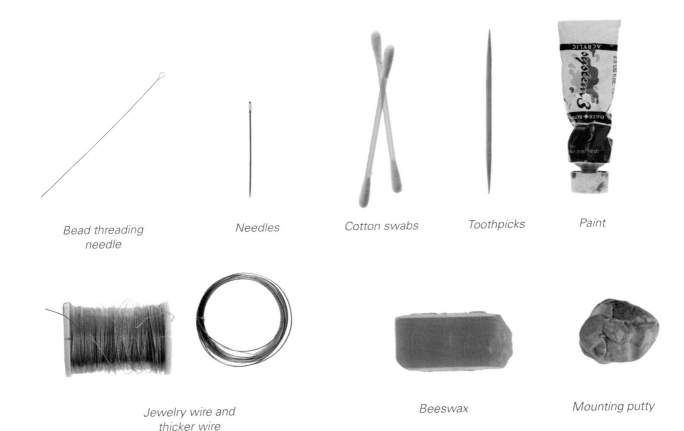

Bead threading
needle

Needles

Cotton swabs

Toothpicks

Paint

Jewelry wire and
thicker wire

Beeswax

Mounting putty

Other handy things for your storage shelves:

Wet and dry sandpaper

Danish oil

Mineral spirits

Varnish

Spray paint

Dust mask

Eye protectors

Masking tape

Rubber mallet

Metal ruler

Cutting mat

Beads and bits:

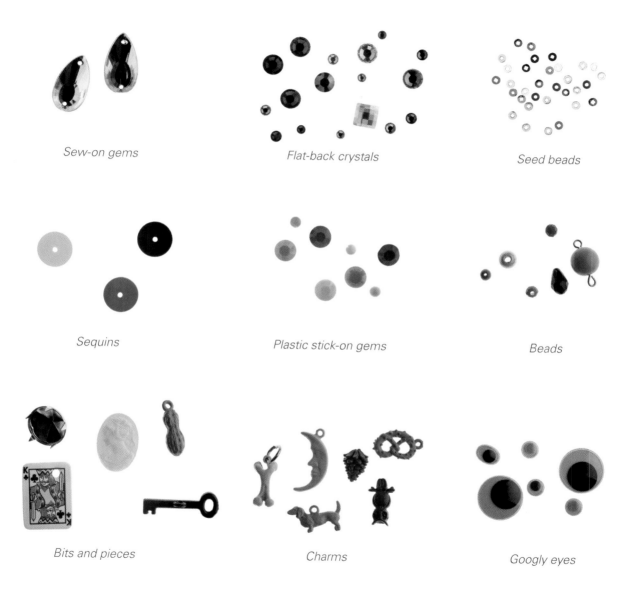

Sew-on gems

Flat-back crystals

Seed beads

Sequins

Plastic stick-on gems

Beads

Bits and pieces

Charms

Googly eyes

FINDINGS

Jewelry is all about joining different bits of things together, and these bits and pieces will help you do just that.

Jump rings are indispensable. They are a simple loop of wire, with a split at the top that's opened with pliers (see page 18). You can connect chains to them, dangle trinkets from them and attach a necklace clasp to them. They come in a variety of sizes and different sorts of metals so it's a good idea to play around with them and find out what works best. You want a jump ring that's strong enough for your chosen make, as flimsy ones will come apart and all your hard work will be undone, and you want one that's the right size—discreet is the way to go for delicate jewelry, but go large for chunky looks. Ideally you want the jump ring to move freely on whatever you're making, so experiment with different sizes until it feels and looks just right.

Here are our favorites:

Tiny jump rings (3 mm) work brilliantly with fine chain. We love the ones that are slightly oval-shaped, with the split along the long edge.

Small jump rings (4 mm) are handy to have around for more delicate projects.

Regular jump rings (6 mm) are used for attaching trinkets, charms and necklace clasps. They're strong enough to link strands of heavier chain and chunky beads, and are just right to act as an end ring on a necklace.

Large jump rings (12 mm) are great with bigger charms or heavy chains.

Bolt clasps
have a tiny spring inside—you push back the little lever, and the spring opens the clasp, which is why it's also known as a spring clasp.

Chains
come in all shapes and sizes. You can reuse old necklaces, recycle junk shop finds or buy new chain from craft shops and online. They come in a variety of types and colors, with odd but lovely names such as silver rhodium, gilt, burnished gold and hematite. Here are our favorites:

Lobster clasps
look just like crustacean claws, and are a fine fastener for a bracelet or necklace. Check that they open and close well, as occasionally the catch can be a little sticky.

Curb chains

A head pin
is like a full stop. It's a length of wire with a disc soldered on one end. Head pins are also used to attach beads to each other, or to the necklace or bracelet chain.

Eye pins
are pieces of wire with a loop on one end that are brilliant for linking beads and charms. They come in a variety of lengths, but you can easily snip them with a wire cutter or you can make your own with fine wire and some round-nose pliers.

Trace chains

Screw eyelets
are found in the DIY shop, and are great for putting up net curtains. But you can also screw them into heavy objects, pop on a jump ring and attach them to the chain of your choice.

Belcher chain

Ball chain

Sam Browne studs
were invented in World War II by a certain Sam Browne, who turned a bullet into a nifty way of fastening together pieces of leather or heavy-duty fabric belts and cuffs. It's known as a "bibble" in Tattyworld.

Bead Tips
are used with crimps, and are threaded onto the end of strings of beads; their loop lets you attach the string of beads to jump rings and clasps.

Crimp beads
are used for finishing ends on strings of beads, and work just like a knot. They are little tubes that are squashed flat with the pliers to form a tight seal to stop the beads from sliding off.

Bead caps
are little domes of metal that can be added on to strings of beads or stuck on top of beads or round objects to turn them into a necklace, with the help of a jump ring.

Kilt pins and safety pins
are great for displaying charms and rosettes on. They come in lots of different sizes, and some even have soldered rings so you can give your trinkets more space. Remember to adorn the bar of the pin that doesn't open, otherwise you won't be able to fasten your new accessory to your lapel.

Beading silks
come in lovely colors and different thicknesses and lengths. Some even have the beading needle already attached! Always choose one that's thin enough to thread through the hole on the bead.

Brooch backs
are the simplest way of transforming a lovely trinket into a piece of jewelry. Check the hinge and clasp of the brooch back to make sure it works before getting busy with the glue.

Cuff links
are lovely and old-fashioned, but you can give them an up-to-date look by gluing small, cool, flat things to the flat disc of this finding.

A barrette
is a great base for creating some snazzy hair accessories. Use a glue gun to fix your decoration on to it. Sewing or wiring on stuff will work as well.

Ring shanks
are, unsurprisingly, necessary to make rings. The ones with the flat discs are perfect for sticking on interesting flat things; the ones with the soldered-on jump rings are great for adding on charms or beads. Most come with an adjustable band, which is perfect if you're making the rings as presents.

Studs
give you options. If you're aiming for gluing something quite large and flat into an earring, go for studs with a soldered-on disc. Bumpy shapes and little things work best with a drilled in post. If you're allergy-prone, splurge on solid silver earring posts; it's no fun having cool earrings but itchy ears.

Clip-ons
And there are always clip-ons if your ears aren't pierced.

Fish hooks
are what you use if you want an earring that dangles. They have a handy small loop, ready for you to attach your chosen object.

In the Mood for Making

Before you start making, it's nice to have a clean and orderly space in which to work, with good light, a comfy chair and a sketchbook to scribble out your ideas.

And it's a good idea to pop a notebook in your bag too, as you never know when inspiration will strike. Here are some of the things that make us think:

Old stuff; tatty things that are tarnished, used and well-loved; thrift stores, rummage sales, flea markets, street finds; old books; historic buildings; music and records; pop culture; old magazines, like the *Golden Hands* craft periodicals and vintage *Vogues*, beautifully bound by Harriet's nan; Rosie's granny's sewing and gardening books, which she wrote and self-published.

Plastic '70s bangles; old children's storybooks; letterpress; pins and buttons; kitsch ceramics; anything giant or miniature; collections of things: postcards, stamps, letters, slides; silk scarves; old watches; old spectacles; world globes; collapsible toys; fans; popper beads…

We love the fact that one girl's trash is another girl's treasure.

First Things First

A length of chain, a clasp
and a few jump rings can
be transformed into a dainty
decoration or a necklace that
sweeps the floor.

There are thick chains, thin chains and medium chains, and the sizes
of jump rings and lobster clasps vary too. As a rule of thumb, the
thicker the chain the bigger the jump rings and the lobster clasps.
The jump ring should comfortably fit the chain, with a bit of wiggle
room. You might have to try out different-sized jump rings to get a
good fit.

Here's how the different sizes of jump ring can connect to different
thicknesses of chain...

Tatty's Top 5
"Chain Songs"

"Chain of Fools"
Aretha Franklin

"Chain Reaction"
Diana Ross

"Chain Gang"
Sam Cooke

"The Chain"
Fleetwood Mac

"Chainsaw"
The Ramones

HOW TO MAKE A BASIC NECKLACE

Cha Cha Chain

You'll need:

A length of fine chain

Ruler

Wire cutters
(or an old pair of scissors)

2 tiny jump rings

2 pairs of flat-nose pliers

2 small jump rings

1 lobster clasp

If you're making a short necklace you'll need approximately 40 cm of chain, for a medium necklace about 60 cm and for a longish necklace your measurement is about 80 cm.

Measure your chain with a ruler and then cut with the wire cutters. You could use an old pair of scissors, but don't use your best ones, as cutting chain will wreak havoc on the blades.

Open the tiny jump rings with the pliers. To do this, grasp one tiny jump ring in one of the pairs of pliers, with the split in the jump ring facing upward. Grab the second pair of pliers in the other hand, at right angles to the first pair, and use it to twist the jump ring apart at the split.

A quarter turn toward you should do the trick. Don't go too far, and don't be too brutal. Carefully attach one end of the chain to your open jump ring and then close the jump ring.

Open the small jump ring using the method above, and pop on the tiny jump ring on the end of the chain. Close the jump ring.

Do the same on the other end of the chain: attach the remaining tiny jump ring, then attach the remaining small jump ring to it and pop on the lobster clasp. Close the small jump ring.

If you want to make a bracelet, do the same wire cutters/pliers/lobster clasp/jump rings thing, but use approximately 18 cm of chain. You might need larger jump rings with thicker chain.

Top TATTY Tip

With some thick chains you can open the links with pliers, rather than snipping them with the wire cutter. With a really fat chain, get out the hacksaw.

LEADERS

To make your necklace adjustable in length you can add a leader. The easiest way to make a leader is to attach a length of medium trace chain to the nonclasp end of the necklace.

A tiny toy wrench saved from a Christmas treat. Anything miniature is great!

Open the nonclasp end of the small jump ring with pliers, slide a short length of trace chain on to the jump ring and then close the jump ring.

Make sure your lobster clasp is a good fit with the medium trace chain, so that it's easy to do and undo anywhere along the length of the leader.

You can also pop a regular-sized jump ring in at any point along the length of your chain, for dramatically different ways of wearing the necklace.

Cut the chain with the wire cutter and then link it to a regular jump ring you can attach the clasp to. If your chain is too fine, add a small or tiny jump ring to both the cut ends of the chain.

When you come to do up your necklace, you can fasten the lobster

clasp to the ring at the end of the necklace, or to the jump ring in the middle of the chain. And you can add a series of regular jump rings on the length of the chain for even more variety. Or you could get really fancy and use beads instead of chain to separate the jump rings (see page 111).

HOW TO MAKE A BOW TIE NECKLACE

It's a Kind of Magic

Vintage shops are full of beautiful dresses. But they are also full of odd little things that you might like the look of, but aren't sure exactly how to go about wearing: nylons that won't stretch enough to fit an actual leg into, but come in pretty packages, and lovely old-fashioned bow ties that are designed to clip to the sort of old-fashioned dress shirts that aren't made anymore. Harriet's granddad was a magician: he swallowed razor blades, and then pulled them out of his mouth on a length of string. He always wore a bow tie. You too can add a dash of magic to your outfit with this bow tie necklace. It's as easy as *hey presto* ... but without the danger of slicing your tongue in half.

You'll need:

1 short 40 cm chain necklace (see page 36)

Wire cutters

2 small jump rings

2 pairs of flat-nose pliers

1 vintage or thrift stores bow tie (with the metal bit on the back)

Optional extras:

1 regular jump ring

2 beads (one big, one small)

1 eye pin

1 head pin

1 pair of round-nose pliers

Make up your necklace using the method shown earlier.

Hold the necklace by the clasp and cut it in half with the wire cutters, opposite the clasp.

Attach a small jump ring to each side of the cut ends of the necklace, using the flat-nose pliers.

Attach the chain to the holes in the back of the bow tie. The jump rings go through the bow tie holes, and the pliers neatly close the jump rings. (If your chain is finer, attach tiny jump rings to each end of the chain, and then attach the small jump rings.)

If you're feeling fancy, you can make it adjustable. With the addition of a regular jump ring your bowtie necklace can go from skimming your chest to nestling at the collar of your shirt. At the nonclasp end of the necklace, 70 mm in, pop in a jump ring, using the wire cutters and pliers technique (see page 36).

You can also add a couple of beads for a decorative flourish, as befits a magician. On the bigger bead, thread on an eye pin. Trim the wire, with the wire cutters, so that there's about 10 mm sticking out. Then bend the wire down at a right angle with the pliers. The next bit is a little tricky, but you'll soon get going with a bit of practice. With the round-nose pliers, roll the wire up into a loop, with tiny twists, rolling away from you. Try to get it to roughly the same size as the loop at the other end. Then, holding each loop with the flat-nose pliers, check that both loops are facing in the same direction. Tweak gently if they aren't.

On the smaller bead, thread on the head pin. Trim the wire and do the loop thing again. Join the beads together through the loops; the small bead is the full stop. Then you can attach them to the nonclasp end of the necklace.

Top TATTY Tip

If the bow tie doesn't have the appropriate hardware on the back, sew two small jump rings to the top corners of the bow tie.

Make sure you've flipped the bow tie over, so you're working on the back. If you sew them about 10 mm in from the top and side edges, they'll be invisible from the front.

Magic.

HOW TO MAKE A LEATHER CUFF

Channel Your Inner '80s Pop Star

When we first started out, we had to create our jewelry in our bedrooms and odd little corners of our flats. Eventually we decided to get a small studio, and went for a long stroll in East London looking for a space. It didn't look too promising until we sat on a wall for a rest at the top of Brick Lane. Opposite us, in the summer sunshine, there was a boarded-up shop. It was a wreck inside, with trash up to our knees, but it had beautiful red-stained glass, and we fell in love with it. We gutted the shop with the help of Harriet's dad, and we moved in with all our equipment—a cutting board, a utility knife and a metal ruler. And that's basically all the stuff you'll need to make this lovely leather cuff.

Make an arrow-headed paper template, using the shape pictured opposite. A good standard fit is about 200 mm in length, but if you have very small or big wrists you'll probably need to play around with the sizing. Add or decrease the length by cutting the template in half and adding in or removing paper to the middle of the strip to make it bigger or smaller, and getting busy with the sticky tape.

Trace the shape of your freshly made paper template on to the leather, with the scribe or the old pen. Trace the slit too.

You'll need:

Paper

Pencil

Scissors

Sticky tape

Length of leather or pleather (The cuff works best with leather that's about 2 mm thick)

A scribe, or something to mark the surface of the leather (A pen that's run out of ink would do the trick)

Cutting mat or board

Metal ruler

Sharp craft knife

Handheld hole punch

Slit: 15 mm

10 mm

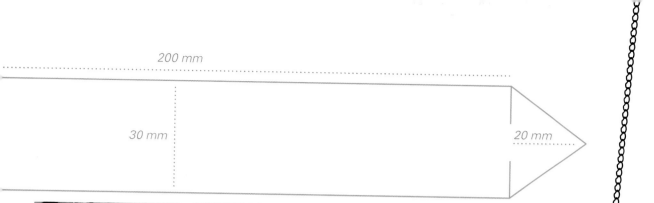

200 mm

30 mm

20 mm

Put the leather on the cutting board, and use the edge of the metal ruler to cut out the shape with the sharp craft knife. BE CAREFUL—don't cut off your fingers!

It might take a few swipes of the knife to get through the leather surface, but aim for nice clean lines, and make sure you've cut right through the leather to avoid hirsute edges.

Use the hole punch and punch 2 mm holes at each

end of the traced slit. Then cut the slit. The first few times you try to pull the arrow head through the slit it might be a bit stiff, but over time the leather will soften, and it'll get easier to fasten.

Oh, and on some leathers the color is not dyed right through, leaving unsightly edges when you make your cuts. You could use specialized dye to stain the edges, but a steady hand and a marker would work too.

Customize Your Cuff

Let your imagination go to town decorating your cuffs. We like brogue detailing and sewing chain down the edges.

HOW TO MAKE A GEM HAIR BAND

Bobby Dazzler

Rosie used to have a part-time job in a vintage shop called Steinberg and Tolkien on the King's Road, and she liked to dress the part. One Friday she was sporting a big, bold, gem-studded hair band when it was spotted by a *Vogue* stylist who was in the shop supposedly browsing for olden-days looks, but who instead fell in love with Rosie's thoroughly modern bright pink hair accessory. She immediately asked to see the Tatty collection. Harriet's mom got straight in her car with her sewing machine (because ours was a bit worse for wear), and we spent the whole weekend sewing gems onto leather and headed to the *Vogue* office on Monday. Before we knew it, Erin O'Connor was wearing a Tatty Devine cuff in *Vogue*'s millennium issue. It was a mad time, but brilliant.

*We love anything
that says "Paris."
Especially if it's shiny.*

You'll need:

Some lush soft leather
approximately 300 mm by 50 mm

Craft knife

2 rulers (one metal)
or anything with a straight edge

Cutting mat or board

Masking tape

Two-part epoxy resin
(see page 54)

Old flyer or playing card

Toothpick

A selection of snazzy sew-on multicolored plastic gems

Leather sewing needle

Buttonhole thread
(in a matching or clashing color)
and thimble

Needlework scissors

Leather/suede
to use as a backing, approximately
310 mm by 60 mm

Contact adhesive

Scrap of old cardboard

Brand-new, fearsomely
sharp craft knife blade

Handheld hole punch

2 lengths of ribbon
about 80 cm long; grosgrain or velvet
are the best (satin is too slippy and
slidey to stay put in your hair)

Optional extras:

Rubber mallet

Scribe

Round coin (to draw around)

Bra slide

Elastic

Think what you want your hair band to look like. You could go crazy with the crystals—haphazard and mad looks fun—or you can take the careful approach, and work out a beautifully decorous design.

Start by cutting a strip of leather, approximately 300 mm by 50 mm (or any size of your choice), using your craft knife, a metal ruler and the cutting board.

If you're going for the crazy gem approach, place the two rulers on either side of the leather strip, 5 mm in from the long sides. Make sure they are straight and parallel, then hold them steady with a bit of masking tape.

Mix up some two-part epoxy resin glue on a flyer or playing card using a toothpick. Leaving 30 mm at each end, stick on as many gems as you can cram in between the two rulers. Use the toothpick to help position them precisely.

If order is your thing, mix up some two-part epoxy resin glue on a flyer or playing card and line the gems up 5 mm from the bottom of the leather, and 30 mm in from the left-hand side. Stick the gems all the way up the strip but stop 30 mm from the other end. Your ribbon will go on here a little later.

Remember to glue your gems with the holes running in a straight line along the length of the band, or your stitching will be all over the place!

This cute spinning top was a present from our artist friend Mark Pawson.

Wait until the glue is dry. Then start a-sewing the gems onto the leather, using the leather needle, thimble and the buttonhole thread. Try to match the color of your thread to the color of your leather, unless you want to make a deliberate contrast statement.

Snip untidy threads with the elegant needlework scissors. It's also worth double-checking that all the gems are sewn securely through all the holes.

The next step is to make a backing to cover up all your careful stitches. Cut the suede 5 mm bigger than the leather, so that's about 310 mm by 60 mm. Stick the suede strip to the cutting board, right-side down, with the masking tape. You can get away with putting a strip of masking tape only on the top and bottom of the suede, but it's best to stick down the sides too. Make sure the suede is taut before you stick it.

Slather the back of the suede with a thin coat of contact adhesive, carefully spreading it on with a bit of old card. Leave no bit uncoated.

Make sure you open a window, or better still, do it outside as the glue is pretty smelly.

Cover the back of the gemmed leather with glue too, making sure it reaches all the way to the edges. Wait for the glue to become dry to the touch—the packet will tell you how long that's going to take.

You may as well get the glue off your fingers while you're whistling and waiting, then there'll be no bad crime-scene gluey prints on the good side of the leather.

Really stubborn bits of glue demand mineral spirits, but warm water and soap generally works, as does facial scrub.

Then join the backs of the suede and the leather together, and press down firmly. Bang it gently with a rubber mallet if you happen to have one around.

Change the blade in the craft knife to a brand-new super-sharp one. This is essential, as one false move and all your hard work will be ruined. No pressure.

Align the metal ruler up against the gems and cut through the leather, as close to the gems as possible, but without cutting any of the stitches, on both the long sides.

Then cut across the ends. For a fancy finish you could round off the corners; this looks especially nice on wide leather bands. A good pair of scissors is just the thing to give you a nice clean edge. To make a curve guideline, use a scribe and a coin on the reverse before cutting.

Punch a 4 mm hole about 10 mm in from the edge of each end of the headband.

Next up is the ribbon. Fold one piece of ribbon in half, and put the fold through one of the holes at the end of the leather band. Thread the ends of the ribbon through the loop you've just made. Pull the tail of the ribbon to tighten the knot.

Do like you just did with the other piece of ribbon, and the hole at the other end of the hair band. Around 80 mm of ribbon on each side will neatly tie your hair band on, but there's nothing to stop you having a cascade of multicolored ribbons sweeping to the floor.

And ribbon isn't the only way to finish off the hair band: leather or a bra-slide-and-elastic combo work too.

For the bra-slide option
First, grab a bra and check how the slide works. You're going to be doing exactly the same with the hair band. Sew the slide to one end of the 10 mm elastic through the middle bar. Thread the other end of the elastic through the hole in the hair band, from back to front, then thread it back through the slide so the slide moves freely along the length of the elastic. This loop is what makes the hair band adjustable. Finally,

thread the other end of the elastic through the other hole in the hair band and sew securely in place.

For the leather option
Assuming you have enough leather left, cut two strips about 10 mm wide and 500 mm long. Tie a knot close to the end of each piece of leather, and thread one into each hole of the head band, with the knot on the inside.

HOW TO MAKE A PHOTOCOPY WATCH BRACELET

Tick Tock, We Can't Stop

It doesn't have to be a watch, but this was one of the first things we laminated. Back then we kept loads of scrapbooks with all kinds of pictures, and photo albums with pages and pages of interesting snaps, as it was tricky to find images. Nowadays there's tons of copyright-free stuff on the Internet, and inspiring images available at a click of the mouse on sites like Tumblr, so you won't be stuck for ideas.

You could go for a diamond bracelet, or a giant stick of chewing gum, or if you have something very precious or sentimental to you that you'd be brokenhearted to lose, you could make a laminate of that, and wear it without fear. Anything will work, but the basic dimensions are about 300 mm by 200 mm.

You'll need:

1 picture of a watch with a strap

Digital camera
or scanner

Photo editing software, if you want to play around with your pic

Computer

Printer

Paper

Copy shop
with a laminating machine

Scissors

A piece of self-adhesive Velcro

Top TATTY Tip

Go wild with the lamination. Collect seed packets and turn your necklace into a garden. Or make a memento charm bracelet, using reduced-size holiday photographs and the faces of your friends.

First find a watch. It can be an image from a magazine, or be the real thing.

Take a photo of the watch. Make sure you shoot it directly from above so that there's no distortion. Or you can scan an image instead.

Upload the photo to your computer, and adjust the image to life size.

Have some fun by zooming in and changing the maker's mark to your name, and the date to a special date—your birthday, a party date, a date date.

Print it out, cut it out and try it on. If you're happy, then hooray. If not, edit the image on screen and reprint. Make a few more, enough to fill up a sheet of paper.

Sashay down to the copy shop with your cutouts. Make sure they stay flat.

Pop the images in between the layers of laminate, leaving a 4 mm gap around each one.

Let the machine do its thing. Head home at top speed and get busy with the scissors.

Carefully cut out your images, 2 mm from their edges, so that the paper

stays snugly sealed between the laminate.

On the strap end of the watch, stick a 20 mm by 20 mm piece of sticky Velcro to the top end. Try it on, to work out where to stick the matching piece of Velcro on the back of the buckle end. When you're pleased with its position, get sticking.

Rosie discovered this beautiful broken watch on a market stall: it's right twice a day.

Sticky Stuff

Here's the Tatty Devine Guide to Glue

We loved white glue at school—it worked brilliantly with glitter, it stuck paper dolls' house furniture together and made the best fake skin (coat both hands with a big splurge of glue, wait for it to dry and then carefully, carefully, carefully peel it off). A DIY horror-film moment. You can have just as much fun with more grown-up glue: dab it to the back of your favorite trinkets, add a brooch back or an earring post and you've made a piece of statement jewelry.

♣ Here's a small but important fact: grease repels glue. Chances are that any thrift store find may well be a bit worse for wear on the dirt front. Luckily a bit of cleaning will sort that out. Warm soapy water is perfect for nonporous materials like glass, plastic, metal and crystals. When everything looks spick-and-span, wipe the area that's going to be glued with mineral spirits, as this'll get rid of any traces of grease that may have been left behind.

♦ Glue also likes a bit of rough. For the glue to do its sticky best it needs a surface with a bit of texture, so on smooth, shiny surfaces get rubbing with a coarse-grade sandpaper, or use a sharp bradawl on the bit that's going to be covered in glue. The official name for this is "keying."

♠ It's a good idea to cover your work surface with old newspaper, as it makes tidying up much easier, and have an old rag or some tissues on hand in case of mishaps. In the case of fast-drying glue, assemble everything you need before you start sticking, and there won't be an *"OH NOOOOOOO!"* moment followed by a scene of you dashing madly around the room looking for that missing something.

♥ Always glue on a level surface, otherwise things could start slipping and sliding as they dry and when you return to your brooch its back might be awry, and not in a good way. If your treasure isn't flat, prop it up with a nugget of mounting putty; that'll level things off nicely.

♣ Even though strong glue will stick most things together, there are exceptions. It's all to do with physics, leverage and force. So even the strongest bond won't keep a ruler stuck to a ring back. Oh, science, you are so important.

♦ Things can get a bit messy, with stray fingerprints and glue trails on your finished piece. Cotton swabs, a soft cloth, mineral spirits and elbow grease will work on nonporous surfaces. If there are huge lumps of glue, you'll need a scalpel or a knife to clean them off. Glue marks on wood can be sanded off, but sometimes the glue will soak into the grain and leave a mark. And be warned: Removing glue from suede is nearly impossible.

♠ Oh, and glue can be a bit smelly, so try to make sure you have some fresh air coming into your workspace. And breathe. *Ahhhhh.*

A Word on Two-Part Epoxy Resin Glue

We love two-part epoxy resin glue, and it is genius; it's probably the most useful glue when it comes to costume jewelry. It sticks most things and it's strong, but there are a few things to bear in mind before you get to work.

First up, always read the instructions. Boring, but essential. Then, always squeeze the exact same amounts out of both tubes. Unless the mix is 50/50 it will NEVER dry. *Never.* Not ever.

Next, it's really important to mix it properly. Our maxim is: "When you think you've mixed it enough—mix it a bit more." Especially the bits of glue that skulk on the edges—make sure they're part of the party. Our tools for this job? A handy toothpick and some old flyers or playing cards. Harriet's brother was also a magician and one of his specialities was swallowing playing cards: He would spit them back out at us when we were trying to make jewelry. The floor and the ceiling were littered with odd jacks and kings and queens, but they were very handy for mixing batches of glue on.

Always make sure you mix enough glue for the job that needs doing, but not too much at once as you only have a few minutes of maximum freshness. So if you are planning on covering your shoes in hundreds of crystals, then mix the glue in small batches on a fresh piece of card stock, using a fresh toothpick each time.

The final tip is the trickiest one: WAIT UNTIL THE GLUE IS DRY. Tempting as it is to wear your new make straight away, try to be patient. That way, you and your new jewelry will have a lasting relationship, rather than coming unstuck immediately. Leave it to dry overnight, if you can.

This was once a teddy bear nose. Our friend Rocky knew we'd love it.

HOW TO MAKE A RADIO BROOCH
Radio Days and Disco Nights

We love Dansettes and transistor radios, and mini musical instruments. We like the way they look, especially if they are red and plastic, but they also remind us how important music is to us. We've always made mix tapes, bought records and CDs and headed off to see our favorite bands play live. Nothing beats turning the dial and hearing the Shangri-Las over the airwaves.

You'll need:

Small plastic radio, or any other cute, flat, plastic item that srikes your fancy

Bradawl

Two-part epoxy resin glue (see opposite)

Old flyer or playing card

Toothpick

Brooch back

Top TATTY Tip

Have you ever lost a brooch when dancing just a little bit too much at a gig or a club? Annoying, very annoying. Here's an easy way to stop that from happening ever again. Do up your brooch, and then squish a bit of mounting putty all around the clasp. Now it won't come undone under even the most dramatic dance-floor duress.

The green lion is another ace find from a flea market rummage box.

Before you start, decide where you want the brooch back to go. It's a good idea to stick it toward the top of your trinket, as that way your finished brooch will nestle nicely against your sweater, without sagging. If you have a fondness for wearing your brooches on your left-hand side, glue the brooch back with the hinge facing right, as this makes it easier to do it up and undo it. If you favor the right, glue the back with the hinge facing left. And if you're sticking the brooch back on vertically, put the hinge at the top, so if the clasp does come undone your brooch will (hopefully) stay pinned to the fabric in time for you to notice.

Clean and key the area on the back of the radio that you're going to glue with the bradawl (see page 53).

Mix up the two-part epoxy resin glue on a flyer or playing card, according to the instructions, using a toothpick—and don't forget the Tatty maxim (see left).

Slather the glue generously to the reverse of the brooch back with the toothpick and then stick the brooch back to the reverse of the little radio.

Leave it to dry.

HOW TO MAKE A GLASS STOPPER PENDANT

Heart of Glass

In a box full of curious smashed glasses and bottle pieces on a stall at Bridport market we came across this perfect glass stopper. We're not sure what it came from—a scent bottle, or a vial to store tears—but it was perfect for a pendant.

We couldn't resist this perky plastic dog. He's just waiting to be made into something cool.

〰

You'll need:

1 head pin

1 bead cap

2 pairs of flat-nose pliers

1 pair of round-nose pliers

1 glass stopper or other rounded tricket

1 cup uncooked rice or couscous

Two-part epoxy resin glue (see page 54)

Old flyers or playing cards

Toothpick

Cotton swab

Mineral spirits

1 regular jump ring

1 chain necklace (see page 36)

We were obsessed with jacks at school; we played every single break time.

〜

Sometimes sticking round or unusual shapes down with some mounting putty works fine but you can also bed your chosen object in a bowl of rice or couscous to keep it level. That will leave both hands free for gluing. Best not to eat the rice afterward though.

First thread the head pin through the bead cap and trim it to 10 mm. With some flat-nose pliers bend the head pin down at a right angle. The next bit is tricky, but you'll soon get the hang of it. With the round-nose pliers, roll the wire of the head pin into a loop by making tiny twists rolling away from you.

Place the bead cap on top of your glass stopper (or another rounded trinket of your choice). Adjust with the pliers for a snug fit. Remove the bead cap again.

Plop the glass stopper into the rice, making sure it's nice and level.

Mix up the two-part epoxy resin glue on a flyer or playing card and apply it generously inside the bead cup with a toothpick. Then pop the gluey bead cap back onto the glass stopper, wiping off any glue that squishes out with a cotton swab. Leave it to dry.

Clean off any glue trails with mineral spirits, using a cotton swab.

Open the regular jump ring with the pliers, attach it to the loop of the bead cap and thread it on to the necklace.

This sticking method will work for anything small and round like a marble or ceramic animal head.

HOW TO MAKE A SAUSAGE DOG BROOCH

Bow Wow WOW

For some people it's all about diamonds, but we prefer going to the dogs: the sausage dogs. We discovered this one (see right) in a thrift store, looking well loved and a little worse for wear, but we just knew he'd look brilliant perched on the lapel of a jacket. Keep your eyes peeled the whole time. You never know when your next brooch is going to find you.

You'll need:

A sausage dog
or any cute trinket

A brooch back

A bradawl

A glue gun

A playing card

Here's a little lost kitten from a thrift store, but now it's at home with us.

Glue guns are great—junk can be jewelry in minutes. They're also ideal for sticking a flat thing to an un-flat thing. Glue's jelly-like consistency is perfect for squeezing into nooks and crannies. Surfaces should still be washed and keyed (see page 53) as glue-gun glue can be a bit rubbery when it cools and it's prone to peeling off shiny surfaces. It's also not particularly neat, so save it for places that won't be on show.

Assemble everything that you need from the get-go. Then decide where you're going to glue the brooch back to the back of the sausage dog. There'll be no time for last-minute decisions!

Key the area you're going to be gluing with the bradawl.

Get the glue gun going.

When it's good and hot, squeeze the first little bit of glue on to the old flyer or playing card, so that the next squirt of glue will be just right.

Now SPEED IT UP. As soon as the glue has left the gun it will start to cool down rapidly—so get it on to the brooch back as fast as you can. Press the hot gluey brooch back on to the dog's side and hold it there. The glue is HOT, so the pin of the brooch back is where your fingers should be. The glue will dry within seconds, ta-da! Super easy and super fast.

Clean off any unsightly blobs with mineral spirits, a cotton swab and elbow grease.

HOW TO MAKE A "SOVEREIGN" RING

Worth Its Weight in Gold

This ring is made from the smallest weight from an old set of weights and scales. They belonged to Harriet's nan, and the two of them spent many a happy hour weighing flour and mixing ingredients. Here you're going to be mixing up glue.

You'll need:

1 brass weight (If your kitchen is lacking scales you can use a coin, a cog or a watch face)

Metal polish or cola (optional)

Mineral spirits

1 disc ring shank

Bradawl

Two-part epoxy resin glue (see page 54)

Old flyer or playing card

Toothpick

If you want a blinging look to the sovereign ring, clean the metal weight with a spot of metal polish. If you don't have any polish on hand, leave the weight in cola overnight, which will, amazingly, also do the job. But old and tarnished looks just fine too.

Make sure the back of the weight is super clean—mineral spirits will do the trick. Clean the ring shank too, and then key both with the bradawl (see page 53).

Mix up the two-part epoxy resin glue on a flyer or playing card, using a toothpick. Slather a generous amount on to the back of the weight and stick it to the ring shank.

Leave to dry overnight.

HOW TO MAKE GLITTER BROOCHES

Party Like the Glitterati

Before we transformed our Brick Lane shop floor into a keyboard, it used to be painted with glitter. It got everywhere, on our shoes and all over our clothes. And there was even more glitter in the air when we cut up the sparkly fabric to make these buttons; we really felt like we were sprinkled in stardust.

Below are four templates you can trace to make a glittery brooch. To make larger ones, you'll need to blow them up on a photocopier or scanner.

You'll need:

Old newspaper

Tracing paper

Pencil

Card stock

Scissors

Glittery fabric

Suede/faux suede or thick felt

Contact adhesive

Rubber mallet (optional)

1 brooch back

Top TATTY Tip

If the shapes are symmetrical, it doesn't matter which way you draw your stencils on the fabric, but if you're working with letters or other non-symmetrical shapes, you'll have to take a little bit more care. Mark the templates with "F" for front and "B" for back. On the glitter fabric the B side should be uppermost, and on the suede the F side. And then everything will be perfectly aligned when you come to gluing.

Contact adhesive is really flexible and works brilliantly on leather or heavy fabric. It's also madly sticky.

Open the window. Spread out old newspapers. Read the glue instructions.

Trace the templates opposite, and then transfer the design onto the card stock. Cut out the card shapes.

On the reverse of the glittery fabric draw around the card shapes. Do the same on the back of the suede or the heavy felt. Cut out the shapes from the fabric.

Spread the contact adhesive thinly and evenly over the wrong sides of both pieces of fabric.

Leave the gluey fabric pieces and wait for a bit, according to the glue instructions.

Deep breath, steady hand. Carefully lay the glitter shape onto the suede shape, wrong sides together. Once the two gluey surfaces meet there's little chance of getting them apart again.

A gift from artist Nervous Stephen. It graced his lampshade, but now it brightens up our studio.

〰

Press them together really hard. If you happen to have a rubber mallet handy, you could give them a whack. Trim around the edges of the shape for a clean, crisp look.

Cut a strip of suede or felt. It needs to be about

3 cm high and the inner width of your brooch back.

Place the suede or felt rectangle onto the reverse of the newly made glitter shape and draw around it. Then spread the glue inside the drawn rectangle and on the reverse of the suede or felt rectangle itself.

Leave for a bit, according to the glue instructions.

Undo the clasp of the brooch back, and place it onto the gluey rectangle on the back of the glitter shape. Then stick the suede rectangle over the brooch back, leaving the pin free.

Press down firmly, leave to dry. And get set to sparkle.

HOW TO MAKE BLINGING CLIP-ON SHADES

Making the Ordinary Extraordinary

We couldn't believe our eyes when our friend John covered his shades in plastic crystals. We were so impressed with his look that we were inspired to make our own. And it's not just glasses that look ace bedecked with crystals, you can stick them on anything—shoes, skirts, pencil cases, bags, dolls' heads, cassette tape boxes...

You'll need:

Clip-on shades

Assorted flatback crystals

Toothpicks

Two-part epoxy resin glue (see page 54)

Old flyer or playing card

Beeswax

Soft cloth

Mineral spirits

Optional extras:

Masking tape

Felt-tip pen

Flashlight

A teeny present from the Duke of Uke, the best ukulele shop in town.

Clean the clip-on shades in warm soapy water.

Pile the different shades and sizes of crystals in front of you and ponder some patterns: think diagonals, concentric circles or swirls, and then imagine them stuck to your shades. You could scan the clip-on shades, print out a life-size image and practice laying out your design; but remember your flat pattern will look different on a curved surface. Take a photo to remind yourself what you're planning to do.

Before you start gluing you could stick masking tape to the reverse of the shades and felt tip your pattern onto the masking tape so you have a guideline to

follow. You might have to shine a light through the lenses to see the felt tip clearly.

Or just throw caution to the wind and get going.

Mix up a small batch of two-part epoxy resin glue and armed with a cut-off toothpick dot the glue on where you want each crystal to gleam. Do a few spots at a time.

Stick a blob of beeswax to the end of another cut-off toothpick. This is a really easy way of picking up the crystals and popping them on the glue.

Pick up the crystals with the cut-off toothpick loaded with beeswax. Keep dotting and sticking until your pattern is complete.

If you're gluing crystals to a curved surface, you'll need to work in stages so that the bit you're gluing is level. Rotate, reposition, leave to dry. And repeat. It sounds more tricky to say than to do.

And then repeat all the steps on the reverse of the shades. Try to keep the crystals perfectly aligned on the back and the front, or you'll have a slim chance of being able to see through them.

Leave to dry, and then polish with a soft cloth and a dash of mineral spirits.

B-B-B-BLING.

HOW TO MAKE JIGSAW PUZZLE EARRINGS

A Little Piece of My Heart

We spent a lot of time on vacation and at art college doing jigsaw puzzles, just staring at the colors and shapes, before getting around to finishing them. Every thrift store has a pile of vintage jigsaws, often with pieces missing, which are perfect for transforming into jewelry. Earrings are simple. Make a pair to match every outfit in your wardrobe.

Top TATTY Tip

Some old and beautiful wooden jigsaws have hidden shapes in the puzzle, like the ones in this picture. If you are lucky enough to discover one, keep it safe, as they can be turned into perfect pendants and brooches.

FRANCE

We love jigsaw puzzles, and we love France.

You'll need:

2 pieces from an old jigsaw
wood if you're lucky, but cardboard will do (cardboard earrings will be a bit more flimsy, and not rainproof!)

Old newspaper

Gloss varnish

Paintbrush

Wet and dry sandpaper

Cloth or a piece of old fabric

Pencil

Silver earring posts

Two-part epoxy resin glue
(see page 54)

Old flyer or playing card

Toothpick

Before you get started, have a Tatty-style ponder of your puzzle. Think about the colors and shapes, and how they'll work as pairs. Look out for interesting bits—faces, flowers or little animals look immediately cute, but you might have to play around with other pieces to come up with a look you like.

When you've decided, lay your pieces out on a newspaper, and give the front of the pieces a light coat of varnish using the paintbrush. Leave them to dry in a nice, clean place: you don't want dust bedevilling all your hard work.

When they've dried, add another coat of varnish, and let that dry. Then varnish the sides too.

Have a quick overview of the dried pieces, and get to work with the wet and dry sandpaper if you spot any flecks, flaws or specks in the freshly varnished surface. Hold the jigsaw puzzle piece with your fingers and put the wet and dry sandpaper on a flat surface and gently rub the puzzle pieces against the sandpaper.

Wipe away the varnish dust with a cloth. The jigsaw pieces should be nice and shiny after two coats, but if you want them to be really glossy, recoat and repeat the steps above.

Turn the pieces over. Pencil mark where you're going to glue the earring post. For the earrings to sit nicely the earring post needs to be glued in the top half of the jigsaw piece.

Mix up the two-part epoxy resin glue with a toothpick—make sure you give it a good old stir. Apply the glue to the earring posts, and then stick the earring posts to the puzzle pieces, using

the pencil marks as a guide. Leave them on a flat surface to dry overnight. If the surface isn't flat, you may find the earring posts have slid right off, and that's not the look you were going for.

Hole-y Moley

We have made necklaces from wooden mobile phone bottle openers and a massive macramé owl wall hanging.

Sometimes the hole is already there, like our Eiffel Tower charm belts. They were made from touristy key rings that we'd discovered in Paris. Rosie used to head off on the Eurostar and haggle in bad French for the best deals, and then we'd whip off the key ring bit and let them dangle from the leather. To test if your ornament will look good as a necklace, thread it on to some ribbon. Some things will flop, hang in an odd way or flip over.

Or they could go sideways, or just be generally lopsided. A jump ring can solve many a problem. Attach a jump ring to the hole in the ornament, and then thread the jump ring to the necklace.

A knitting gauge is always handy, especially when it's this super cute.

A lovely keepsake from a special cake.

A find from a Parisian flea market. Ooh-la-la.

HOW TO MAKE A TAPE MEASURE ROSETTE

Inch by Inch...

We've always loved tape measures. In our sewing kits are old vintage tape measures, in shades of baby blue and pale yellow, which once belonged to our grannies and our moms. Every time we see one in a thrift store we have to buy it to add to our collections, even if we know we're never going to use them to actually measure anything. They're perfect for making a fluttering curtain for a doorway, but with a bit of folding and pinning they can also be transformed into pretty star-shaped rosettes, which will get people talking. Rosie was even given a free steak by the local butcher when she wore her rosette into his shop, so impressed was he with her dapper brooch.

You'll need:

1 tape measure

Handheld hole punch
(If you don't have a hole punch, you can use the prong of the kilt pin to poke the holes)

2 brads

Pair of sharp scissors

1 kilt pin or large safety pin

1 pair of flat-nose pliers

Optional extras:

Small piece of felt

Blob of contact adhesive

Embroidery thread and a needle

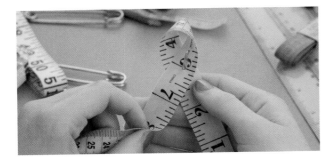

Smooth the tape measure out, and go to work on the inches side. You'll be using both metric and imperial measurements in this make, so pay attention!

Start by punching 2 mm size holes at 3-inch intervals along the middle of the tape measure, starting at number 3, and stopping at number 33. Now make three more holes at numbers 35, 37 and 39. As you're working, give the hole punch a little twist as you squeeze down, so that the little circle of plastic will pop out the back as you press.

Grab hold of one of the brads, and poke it through the tape measure at number 3. The pinhead goes on the centimeters side.

Now for some loops. Give the tape measure a little twist and then pop the newly made loop onto the brad at hole number 6. Oh, and make sure that the inches side of the tape measure is ALWAYS facing upward; this is the side where the brad prongs are sticking out.

Keep twisting and popping the loops onto the paper fastener at every hole, at those 3-inch intervals, and always heading and twisting in the same direction.

When you've made five loops, do a little preening, and even them out into a nice star shape.

If it is not a nice star shape you have probably not twisted the same way every time. Undo and start over.

And off you go again. Make another five loops in the same way. The points of this star should fall between the points of your first star. A bit more preening wouldn't go amiss.

Hooray, you've arrived at number 33 on the inches side of the tape measure. Now for the smaller inner loops. Make three smaller loops, and pop them, one after the other, on the brad. This time you're not heading for the stars; a triangle is the shape you're after. This is going to be the center of the rosette. Snip off the excess tape measure with a pair of sharp scissors, at 39¼ inches. Cut at a jaunty angle, because it looks pretty. Don't throw it away: you're going to need it in a sec.

Take hold of the second of the brads, and push it through the center of the rosette. This will make the first brad pop out, and (ta-da!) the prongs will now be at the back.

Cut 6 inches from the excess snipped-off bit of the tape measure. Make sure you use the end with the metal bit, and fold it in half. Give it a little twist, so that the two strands sit apart, and at an angle. This is the tail of the rosette. Drape the strands over the bar of the kilt pin that doesn't open, otherwise when you come to pin it to the neck of your snazzy sweater you won't be able to!

Grab the hole punch again, and punch a hole through both strands of the tail, close to the kilt pin. Then pop the folded tail, with the kilt pin, onto the reverse of your rosette.

Squash the prongs of the brad down firmly with the pliers, so that everything is held securely in place. You're mostly done, but for a prettier finish you could:

Glue a piece of felt over the back of the brad, with contact adhesive. This will stop it snagging your jumper. If you're feeling really fancy, sew your name onto the felt before you glue; it'll look just like a lovely label. Or you could even embroider a message

onto the felt if you're giving the rosette as a gift.

If you're working with centimeters, here's where you punch the holes: start at 8 cm, then punch every 8 cm, but STOP at 88 cm, and punch three extra holes at 93, 98 and 103. Cut the tape measure at 104 cm—the tail should be about 20 cm long.

Top TATTY Tip

Your rosette could become an ornament for a necklace. Make up the rosette as above, but call a halt before you add on the tail and the kilt pin. Grab hold of a pair of round-nose pliers and, instead of pushing apart the prongs on the brad, smooth them together with the pliers. Bend the prongs down with the pliers, and then roll them up in a tight little circle. Then attach a jump ring and thread it to a necklace.

With a bit of practice you could make a rosette in ten minutes. And you don't just have to use tape measures. What about ribbon rosettes? You'll need to pencil the measurements onto the ribbon, and then get looping. Bear in mind if you're using tiny ribbons, the holes should be closer together, and further apart if you're working with a massive ribbon.

And if you want the rosette to be mega-large, use ribbon that's much longer than 39 inches and keep making loops until the rosette is as big and fat as an ornamental cabbage, but not so big that you can't close the brad. Thinner ribbon will give you the best result. Try these measurements for a brilliant effect on about 2.5 meters of 20 mm ribbon: 6 holes every 10 cm, 5 every 9 cm, 5 every 8 cm, 5 every 7 cm, 5 every 5 cm and 3 at 3 cm.

Top TATTY Tip

You could continue the centimeters and inches theme and make yourself a tape measure belt to match your tape measure rosette. Get an old white belt and a black permanent marker, and draw on the inches by hand. It doesn't have to be accurate; in fact the further apart your inches are, the narrower your waist will appear when you do the belt up.

This vintage tape measure was Rosie's granny's.

HOW TO MAKE A SHRINKY NECKLACE

Good Things Come in Small (Chip) Packages

We ate so many bags of cheap chips when we made these shrinky necklaces to sell in the shop. Hundreds! And we became obsessed by the packaging, and the amazing graphics on noodle packets and candy wrappers from international markets. One day we found an ancient empty chip packet—hedgehog flavor—under the floorboards and it was like discovering gold!

You'll need:

Old food packets (not foiled or metallic)

Greaseproof paper

Baking sheet

Damp dish towel (in case of fire-related emergencies)

Old dish towel

Handheld hole punch

1 regular jump ring

2 pairs of flat-nose pliers

1 chain necklace (see page 36)

A Moldy Peaches ticket, the perfect band to shrink chip bags to.

〜

Eat the contents of the packets while making up the necklace. Salt and vinegar chips, yum.

Make an envelope with the greaseproof paper and pop your food packet inside it. Set your oven to a medium heat and let it warm up a bit. Put the envelopes on a baking tray and put it in the oven. Don't wander off. The packets will start to shrink and curl up but you don't want them to burn or blister, so keep an eye on proceedings.

As soon as you think they've shrunk enough, remove the baking sheet and quickly pop a folded dish towel on top of the envelope and then slam your hand down on it to flatten your shrinkies. BAM! Such a satisfying noise.

Don't worry if it goes wrong the first few times you attempt it, as there's a bit of a knack to it. Practice on easy-to-come-by stuff, and when you've mastered the art, go to work on your carefully hoarded vintage packages.

Now decide how you want your shrinky to dangle. If you punch a hole in the corner it'll hang aslant, but if you punch a hole in the top center it'll dangle straight down. Use the hole punch to make the hole when you've chosen its position.

Open a regular jump ring with the pliers and thread the packet onto the jump ring and then the jump ring to the necklace. Close with the pliers.

HOW TO MAKE A HORSE BRASS NECKLACE

Make up the necklace.

Open the large jump ring with the pliers.

Thread the chain and the brass palette through the jump ring, and then close the jump ring with the pliers.

Look what happens when you don't use a jump ring (see left).

Bold as Brass

Any horse-brass-type ornament would look good for this necklace—anchors or nautical shapes are lovely, but you might be lucky enough to find one of a local cathedral or castle. But do go for one that has holes in it already, as they're really too heavy to glue.

You'll need:

1 pendant-length brass necklace
(approximately 80 cm long, see page 37)

1 large jump ring

2 pairs of flat-nose pliers

1 brass palette or similar horse brass

An old horse brass from the Isle of Wight, where Rosie grew up.

HOW TO MAKE A MUSICAL NOTE CHARM BRACELET

Take Note

When we first started Tatty Devine, we'd pile into Rosie's old Mini and scour cake shops across the land, looking for cool decorations. We found some great little decorations in a shop in Portsmouth, which we made into charm bracelets and earrings, but we also love these musical notes, which we bought from one of our favorite shops, Party, Party in Dalston—so good they named it twice.

For a simple project, choose shapes wih holes in already like these.

You'll need:

18 cm trace chain bracelet (see page 36)

Several treble clef (or semiquaver) cake decorations

2 pairs of flat-nose pliers

Regular jump rings, one for each "charm"

Make up the bracelet.

Try it on. Just right? Hooray. Too tight, add a leader. Too loose, get the wire cutters out.

Count the links on the chain so you can space out your cake charms nice and evenly. For example, if your bracelet has 25 links, then put the notes on links 3, 7, 11, 15, 19 and 23.

Grab hold of the pliers and the jump rings and attach the charms along the length of the bracelet.

You can add as many as you like, or keep adding to it as you find more fab stuff with holes in it.

Top TATTY Tip

If you want your notes to be black, then get the spray paint out. Open the window, or head outside. Get rid of dirt or grease with warm, soapy water, and let the notes dry out. When they're dry, spray the front with undercoat, which helps paint stick to plastic. Let it dry and then spray the back. Let that dry too. Then get going with the black spray paint. Cover the front, let it dry and then spray the back and let that dry too. Make up a jaunty tune to accompany your back-to-black musical notes.

Drill Bits and Pieces

Don't fear the drill. You need to be careful, but once you get going you can put a hole in almost anything—just not your fingers!

A cast-off piece of wood discovered in Pam's place in Bridport.

♣ Safety goggles are always a good idea, as is tying your hair back. Long hair twisted around a drill is no fun. Ditch scarves, ties and any dangly necklaces and bracelets too, before you start drilling.

♦ Cover your mouth with a mask: plastic or wood dust is not nice to breathe in.

♥ If you're worried about scratching the surface of your lovely trinket, smooth on a bit of masking tape, and pencil mark where you want to drill. Then whip it off when you're done.

♠ Hold the items that you're drilling firmly so they don't spin out of control, and always drill straight down. Take your time.

♥ Things can get hot, so if possible use a clamp or a vice, as that way your fingers won't get burned. Ouch.

♣ Invest in some beeswax. It's a great lubricant: dab the drill bit with it and it'll make everything smoother.

A Rough and Ready Guide to Drill Bit Sizes

Your drill bit size is related to the size of the jump rings you're using, and the thickness of the thing you're going to drill. If you're drilling through thin things, like guitar picks, go for a drill bit that's slightly bigger than the wire the jump ring is made of. So with a 5 mm jump ring that's made of 1.6 mm wire, go for a 1.8 mm drill bit. Or if you're drilling through something that's thicker than 4 mm, use a bigger jump ring and a 3 mm drill bit. But the best way to work out your jump-ring-to-drill-bit relationship is to test it out. Drill on a scrappy bit of something that's the same thickness as your chosen object. The jump ring should move freely in the drilled hole, so adjust the size of the jump ring and the drill bit until you find a good fit. Oh, and if you're drilling into something flat, think about where the hole should go before you drill. Too close to the edge, and it'll snap; too far away, and the jump ring won't reach. With the simple addition of a hole, a junk shop find can be transformed into a cool Friday night accessory. There's a whole world of ornaments out there that would be better as jewelry, rather than gathering dust on the mantelpiece. As Rosie often says: "Make a shelf of yourself."

Puzzles are great for long journeys, especially if your phone runs out of batteries.

HOW TO MAKE A GUITAR PICK BRACELET AND NECKLACE

I Should Be So Plucky, Plucky, Plucky...

Guitar picks were one of the first "found" objects that we turned into jewelry. It was quite a revelation! Harriet shared a Brick Lane flat with a band, and the boys left guitar picks everywhere.

When we had cleared out their stash, we headed down to Denmark Street and braved the cute rock boys who worked behind the music shop counter. It was great listening to them recount stories about the gigs they'd been to the night before and how hungover they were, while we picked out what color guitar picks we wanted.

It made us want to be in a band too. We even had a few rehearsals in the Brick Lane studio, though we never played a gig. But every time Rosie went to see a band she used to steal their picks from the stage and add them to her charm bracelet.

If you can't nick them from a band, you can buy all sorts online. Picks come in loads of bright colors, but there are also tortoise shell ones, clear ones, wooden ones and ones printed with pictures—an endless array of loveliness.

Here are the instructions for a charm bracelet and necklace, but once you've got these skills under your belt, the world's your oyster. Go crazy and put guitar picks on anything you can think of: earrings, belts, key rings, light pulls...

There are hundreds of different color picks in the Denmark Street music shops.

A much-prized pick stolen from our housemates, the band Duke Spirit.

You'll need:

Assorted guitar picks

Pen or pencil

Scrap wood
(or something you don't mind drilling holes in)

Drill

1.8 mm drill bit

2 pairs of flat-nose pliers

Regular jump rings
(one for each pick)

For the bracelet:

A thick trace chain bracelet
(see page 36)

For the necklace:

A 40 cm necklace
(see page 36)

Make up the bracelet.

Play around with the picks to see which colors work best together. Once you have got your colorway going on, think about how you want the picks to hang. They'll dangle differently depending on where you drill. We've chosen to drill in the middle.

Drill one pick at a time. Pen or pencil a dot where you want the hole to go. Place the scrap wood on a sturdy surface, and then firmly hold the pick down with your pointing finger. Drill a hole, and pick off any little bits of plastic that might have been left behind. You want nice, clean circles.

Oh, and if you drill the top and the bottom of the pick, you'll be able to link more than one pick together.

If you don't have a drill, you could have a go with a hole punch. It's trickier, though, as picks have a tendency to crack under hole-punch pressure. Best solution? Find a DIY friend and borrow their drill. You can make them a guitar pick accessory as a thank-you present.

Now for a little spacey interlude. Count the links on your chain. For the picks to hang nicely, it's important to hang them on the same side of the link all the way along the bracelet. So, for example, if your chain is 25 links long, start in 3 links from the end, and put jump rings on every other link, so you can attach 11 evenly spaced picks. If you want your bracelet to be less jangly, then put jump rings on links 3, 7, 11, 15, 19 and 23, and attach 6 picks. Or you could go for a mega pick bracelet with one on every link, but make sure that all the links are always on the same side of the chain. OK?

Lay out the picks in the order you want them attached to the bracelet. Grab both pairs of pliers and the regular jump rings and attach the picks to the chain.

Make up the necklace.

Mark up the picks and drill holes in them, as described above. Attach a regular jump ring to each pick and close it up tightly with the pliers.

Thread the picks on to the chain. Make sure the picks are facing out the right way.

Top TATTY Tip

Guitar pick jewelry is always cool, and handy too! If you're the guitarist in a band and you're missing a pick, you can always unthread one and strum on.

HOW TO MAKE A KEYBOARD NECKLACE

I'm with the Band

We love, love, love keyboards. We've made keyboard belts and ties, and the floor of the Brick Lane shop has a keyboard painted on it. It makes us think of the Blondie LP *Parallel Lines*, with Debbie Harry in a white dress, the boys in the band dressed in black and a black-and-white-striped background. Have your own musical moment with this pitch-perfect keyboard necklace.

You'll need:

60 cm necklace (see page 36)	Masking tape
1 small toy piano	Pencil
Small screwdriver	Drill
Hacksaw	1.8 mm drill bit
File	Scrap wood
Wet and dry sandpaper	2 pairs of flat-nose pliers
	Regular jump rings (one for each piano key)

Make up your necklace.

Take the toy piano apart and remove the white and black keys with the small screwdriver.

If the keyboard keys are molded together, separate them by sawing through the plastic with the hacksaw.

File off any sharpness and then smooth the edges with the wet and dry sandpaper. Put the sandpaper face up on a flat surface, and gently rub the piano keys against it.

Turn the keyboard the wrong side up, cover it with masking tape and mark where you want to drill with the pencil.

Fit the drill with a 1.8 mm drill bit and then carefully drill through each key. Remember to put scrap wood under the keys so that you don't accidentally drill through the kitchen table. When you've finished drilling, remove the masking tape.

Lay the piano keys out the way you want them to hang on the necklace.

Holding the necklace at the clasp, work out where the center of your necklace is. Pop the middle piano key on to the center of the necklace with a regular jump ring and the pliers.

Working from the center out in each direction add a jump-ringed piano key on every other link, on the same side of the chain, until all the charms are used up.

This mini keyboard reminds us of Snoopy cartoons, with a soundtrack by Schroeder.

HOW TO MAKE AN OLD COIN NECKLACE

Find a Penny and Pick It Up

When we found this threepenny bit, we had to make it into a necklace. But any old coin would work—old pieces look massive compared to modern ones, and an old franc necklace would be perfect attire for listening to Serge Gainsbourg, or watching *À Bout de Souffle* on the sofa.

You'll need:

1 old coin

Masking tape

Pencil

Scrap wood

Bradawl

Hammer

Clamp

Drill

High-speed steel 2 mm drill bit

Beeswax block

60 cm fine chain necklace (see page 36)

1 jump ring

2 pairs of flat-nose pliers

Who doesn't love free stuff, especially when it's given to us by friends?

Peruse your glorious coin and decide where you're going to drill. Head or crest to the front? Focus on the lettering? These are the things you need to consider before making a hole.

You'll need to drill at least 2 to 3 mm in from the edge of the coin. The hole is going to be 2 mm in diameter, so you need a bit of leeway. It's a good idea to stick a little bit of masking tape to the coin and mark it with a pencil, as a guide. Handily the masking tape will also help to protect your coin if your drilling hand slips when you get going.

Align the tip of the bradawl with your pencil mark and bash the bradawl with the hammer. This little hole

will act as a guide for the drill bit.

Pop the bit of scrap wood underneath the coin, and clamp them together to a sturdy surface or a workbench. The coin gets really hot when you're drilling, so the clamp will save you from burned fingers.

Start the drill, and dip the tip of the drill bit in the beeswax block. You'll need to do this at regular intervals. Start to drill the hole in the coin, slowly and gently. If you're doing it right, you should see little flecks of coin spreading over the workbench; if not, then push a little bit harder, but always remember the beeswax, and keep the pace slow. Too much friction and heat will temper the coin and make it harder to drill.

When you reach the far side of the coin, pull the drill out while it's still rotating so that it doesn't get stuck.

Unclamp the coin, and hey! A hole. Careful, it might be hot.

Attach it to the necklace with the jump ring and the pliers.

But don't stop there: get drilling and add more treasure trove coins to the necklace. Or you could drill holes in each end of the coins and link them together with jump rings to make coin chain bracelets or necklaces or belts.

Top TATTY Tip

If you want to make a coin necklace, but are put off by all the drilling, head to the DIY shop and pick up one of these.

Clean and key the back of the coin (see page 53) and the back of the D-loop. Mix up some two-part epoxy resin glue (see page 54), stick them together and leave them to dry overnight. Use the handy little wire to thread it to your necklace.

HOW TO MAKE A WOODEN MUSHROOM NECKLACE

Knock on Wood

We are nuts about anything that has a wood effect. Show us a wood-look belt, fabric or sticky-back plastic and we're there. But we LOVE real wood too. Owls, squirrels, birds, toadstools—basically anything that you find in a woodland that's been carved out of wood—make our hearts skip a beat. Especially when they're transformed into necklaces. You can paint them. Or keep them au naturel with polish and varnish.

Harriet's giant clothespin, bought from a garage sale in Joshua Tree, USA.

You'll need:

A small wooden object
(like our lovely mushroom)

Wet and dry sandpaper

Danish oil

Paintbrush

Soft cloth

Pencil

Drill

0.8 mm drill bit

Two-part epoxy resin glue
(see page 54)

Old flyer (or playing card)

Toothpick

1 screw-in eyelet

1 pair of flat-nose pliers

Shoelaces or ribbon

Wash away the wood's grubbiness with some warm soapy water.

If it looks a little lackluster, rub it down with wet and dry sandpaper, and add a little Danish oil to the grain. Danish oil gives a lovely, light satin sheen to wood, and it's subtler than varnish because it seeps into the wood, rather than just coating it. Paint it on to the wood, use a soft cloth to remove the excess oil and then rub some more so it gently glows.

Pencil mark where you're going to drill on top of the mushroom.

Drill a pilot hole, about 3–4 mm deep, straight down. Dust off any sawdust. This hole is a guide for the screw-in eyelet, so the pilot hole should be smaller than the screw, and with luck it will prevent the wood from cracking as you're not forcing the metal through the grain.

Mix up the two-part epoxy resin glue on a spare flyer or playing card using the toothpick. Put a blob of glue on the end of the eyelet, pop the eyelet into the drilled hole and twist it. Keep turning the eyelet until it's snugly fitted into the wood. Use pliers to hold the eyelet if it feels tricky.

Thread the shoelace through the eyelet and fasten it with a knot. Make sure it is long enough to go over your head so you don't have to undo it.

A pack of vintage buttons
that reminds us of dice.
We love how they look.

HOW TO MAKE A TINY FRUIT MACHINE DICE NECKLACE

Tutti Frutti

We've whiled away many a rainy hour with board games, jigsaw puzzles and Boggle tournaments. And any time we saw a travel chess set, we bought it; the tiny pieces made perfect dangly earrings or charms. The same holds true for stray pieces, like this neat little fruit dice, from those wet-weather board games. Find a random assortment of bits and bobs and get drilling.

You'll need:

1 fine-chain necklace (see page 36)	Two-part epoxy resin glue (see page 54)
1 small, cute object (we've used a vintage die)	Old flyer (or playing card)
Drill	Toothpick
0.8 mm drill bit	Bowl of uncooked rice
Mounting putty	1 regular jump ring
Wire cutters	2 pairs of flat-nose pliers
1 eye pin	

Small and cute objects need small and cute findings. An eye pin—the more delicate cousin of the screw-in eyelet—is the way to go.

Make up the necklace.

Decide which corner of the die you want to drill, depending on how you want it to hang.

Hold the die and drill down about 4 mm. If it feels wobbly, put a blob of mounting putty on a flat surface and put the dice on top of that to keep it steady.

Using the wire cutters, snip the eye pin so there's around 4 mm of wire left.

Top TATTY Tip

You could set eye pins in the opposite corners of lots of dice, and string them together to make a pretty bracelet.

Pop the eye pin into the drilled hole to try it for size. The loop on the pin should be flush with the die. If it isn't, do a bit more snipping with the wire cutter.

Mix up the two-part epoxy resin glue on a flyer or playing card, using the toothpick. Dip the eye pin end into the glue and then pop it back into the drilled hole.

Make sure you set the eye pin in so that your pendant will hang to the front and not twist around.

Leave to dry overnight, standing upright in a bowl of rice.

When it's dry, open a small jump ring with the pliers and attach it to the eye of the eye pin, and then thread it onto the necklace.

Making a Spectacle of Yourself

We Love Glasses...

Rosie used to make works of art with them but she only used the lenses, so there were loads of frames scattered around the studio. It made us wonder what else you could do with them. Years later they inspired our acrylic glasses necklaces, but why not make your own DIY version, and look super-smart? There's nothing like a bit of secretary chic.

Eye eye, just waiting for a dab of glue and a brooch back.

HOW TO MAKE A SIMPLE GLASSES NECKLACE

Fix Up, Look Sharp

Try hunting for old glasses at yard sales or thrift stores. We especially favor frames from old-style glasses, vintage shades, cat's-eye spectacles, and the sort of glasses that Jarvis Cocker or your granny would wear.

A saucy dart flight from a trophy shop in Whitstable, bought on a very rainy day.

You'll need:

- 1 pair of old glasses
- Soft cloth
- Cotton swabs
- Toothpicks
- Bench vice
- Hacksaw
- Small flat file
- Drill
- 1.2 mm drill bit
- Two-part epoxy resin glue (see page 54)
- Old flyer (or playing card)
- 2 small screw-in eyelets
- 60 cm necklace (see page 36)
- Wire cutters
- Regular jump rings
- 2 pairs of flat-nose pliers

Optional extras:

Tiny, flat-back black crystals

Old spectacle frames are often really dirty when you first come across them, like all the best treasure. But don't be put off: A good clean will get rid of years of accumulated grime. Warm, soapy water is the best. Harsh cleaners can corrode some old types of plastic and may strip away any lovely details that are painted or printed on the frames.

Use a soft cloth to avoid scratches and get busy with toothpicks and cotton swabs to get into all the nooks and crannies.

When the clean-up is done and dusted, remove the arms of the glasses. Hold the glasses securely in a vice and, using the hacksaw, cut

through the hinges as close to the frame as possible.

Using the file, smooth off any sharp edges. These will be against your skin so the smoother the better.

Hold the frames in the vice, and drill a hole approximately 3 mm deep into the top corner of the glasses frame, using the 1.2 mm size drill bit. Make sure you don't hit the lenses or the metal inside the frames. Do the same on the other side.

Mix up the two-part epoxy resin glue on a flyer or playing card, using a toothpick. Dab a small blob of glue onto the screw-in eyelets and then screw them into the holes on the frame. Leave to dry.

Make up the necklace; it looks best if it is long enough for you to hold the chain up to your face. Hold up the necklace by the clasp and, using the wire cutters, cut it in half, opposite the clasp.

Attach the chain to the regular jump rings with the pliers, and then the jump rings to the eyelets. Pop it over your head, and voilá— simple library chic.

Plain and simple is lovely, but if you want something a bit more snazzy, there's a world of possibilities. Cartoon eyes look great.

You need masking tape, two-part epoxy resin glue and its accoutrements, and some little, tiny, flat-back black crystals. (Not only will they look amazing, they

also make a genius tongue twister—tiny, flat-back black crystals, tiny, flat-back black crystals...)

Have a quick peruse of a cartoon for some inspiration. Stick masking tape pupil shapes to the back of each lens, cartoon-style. On the front of the shades, carefully glue the black crystals, following the masking tape shape (see page 66 for gluing instructions).

You'll go a bit googly-eyed with all the sticking, but it'll be so worth it. Leave to dry overnight. Peel off the masking tape, clean any stray blobs of glue with mineral spirits and cotton swabs, and you're ready for your starry close-up.

HOW TO MAKE A PEARL GLASSES NECKLACE

The World Is Your Oyster

You'll need:

1 pair of old glasses (children's work well)	Two-part epoxy resin glue (see page 54)	Superglue
Soft cloth	Old flyers (or playing card)	Needlework scissors
Cotton swabs	2 small screw-in eyelets or cut-off head pins	4 bead tips
Toothpick		81 4 mm pearls or beads
Bench vice	1 packet of no. 10/0.9 mm natural silk beading thread (Buy the sort that has the needle already attached)	4 eye pins
Hacksaw		Wire cutters
Small flat file		1 pair of round-nose pliers
Drill	4 crimps	1 head pin
0.8 mm drill bit	2 pairs of flat-nose pliers	6 small jump rings
		1 lobster clasp

If you can find an old pair of children's glasses for this necklace, they will give you a pretty, petite look. If not, adult specs will still look spectacular.

Follow the instructions up to attaching the chain in the How to Make a Simple Glasses Necklace make (see page 107).

Take the beading silk and tie a knot 10 mm from the end. Thread on a crimp right up to the knot.

Squash the crimp with the flat-nose pliers as above. Dab a tiny blob of superglue onto the knot. Let it dry, then snip off the thread end, as close to the knot as you can, with the needlework scissors.

Thread on a bead tip, and squish it round the crimp.

Things are about to get knotty. Thread on 38 pearls, leaving about 10 cm before the bead tip, so that you've got room to tie a knot on the string without the pearls getting in the way.

Slide one pearl down to the bead tip, and tie a knot in the silk, right up tight to the bead so it's nice and secure. Use the end of the silk with the bead tip on for working the knot.

Slide the next pearl down to the freshly tied knot, and tie another knot as close as you can get, after the new pearl. Make sure the knots are really tight, and the pearls are as close as possible. Keep on sliding and knotting until there's only one pearl left. This time it's not a knot you're after, but a bead tip.

Thread the bead tip on, followed by a crimp. Hold the crimp firmly with the tip of the pliers, but don't squash it. Next, pull on the silk beading thread, and push down with the pliers so that the bead tip and the crimp are not even a hair-breadth away from the last pearl. Happy? Then squash that crimp!

Tie a knot right next to the crimp, dab a spot of superglue on to the knot, wait until it's dry and then trim the thread with the needlework scissors. Then squish the bead tip around them so it's all nicely sealed in place.

Make yourself another strand of pearls to match the first one.

Gently pull on the strands of pearls to unkink any kinks. Now for a fancy fastening. Grab hold of the remaining five pearls, plus four eye pins and one head pin. Pop one pearl onto one eye pin. Trim the wire, with the wire cutters, so that there's about 10 mm sticking out. Then bend the wire down at a right angle with the flat-nose pliers. With the round-nose pliers roll the wire up into a loop, with tiny twists, rolling away from you. Try to get it to roughly the same size as the loop at the other end.

As a rough rule, the closer the wire is to the handle of the round-nose pliers, the bigger the loops are going to be, so for a large loop grip the wire toward the handles, and for a smaller loop grip the wire toward the tip.

Then holding each loop with the flat-nose pliers, check that both loops are facing in the same direction. Tweak gently if they aren't. Repeat with three more pearls.

Top TATTY Tip

You could make this pearly necklace for your real glasses. Make one very long strand of pearls using this technique, and add regular jump rings to each end. Head to the opticians and buy two rubber eyeglass holders, and attach your strand of glam pearls to them.

Pop the fifth pearl onto the head pin, trim and roll the wire in exactly the same way.

Link all these pearls together with five small jump rings to make a little string of pearls. And then join the jump ring end of the little string of pearls to one of the main strands of pearls. If your bead tip is lacking a loop, roll up its wire in the exact same way as the head pin.

On the other strand, attach the lobster clasp with the last small jump ring. The clasp should comfortably fit anywhere on to the little string of pearls, which means your necklace is adjustable. Hooray.

Then attach a pearl strand to each side of the glasses frame, to the screw-in eyelets, making sure that the clasp is in your right hand when you put the necklace on (assuming you're right-handed). Aah. Pretty as a picture.

Make an accessory of an accessory. These tiny specs belonged to a toy doll.

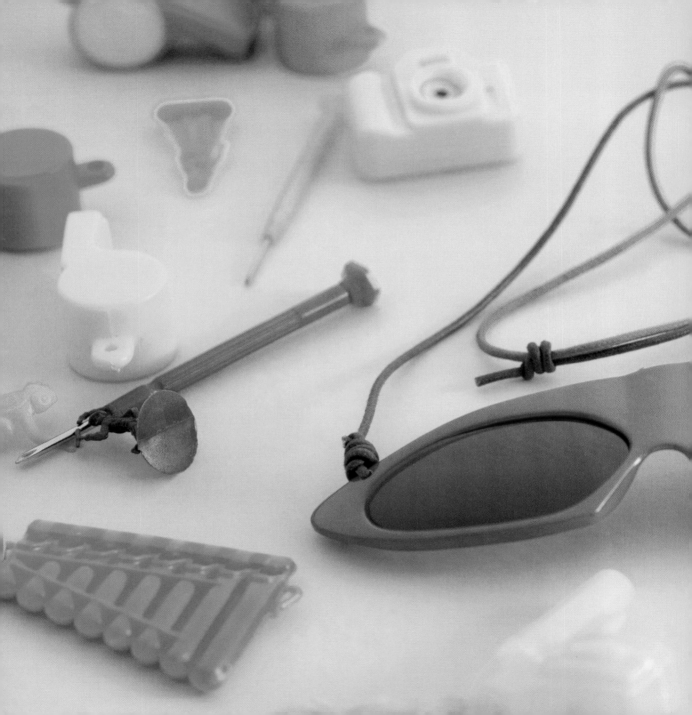

HOW TO MAKE A SNAZZY SUNGLASSES NECKLACE

Shady Lady

Modern sunglasses are often molded, so you can unscrew the arms at the hinges with a small screwdriver. Tempting as it is to thread the shoelaces through these holes, don't, as your necklace will hang downward, rather than be pert and perky.

You'll need:

1 modern pair of molded sunglasses

Drill

2 mm drill bit

Shoelaces or cord

Superglue

Needlework scissors

Get the drill out. Handily these types of glasses have a lot of frame, and no internal metalwork, so you can drill straight through the frames.

Drill a hole each side of the frame with a 2 mm drill bit, or slightly larger depending on the laces you find.

Here's where we get fancy with knots. The hangman's noose is the one you'll be using.

Getting the tension right can be tricky at first, but with a bit of practice, it'll all be fine. Thread the cord through the hole in one side of the glasses.

The leading end should be 150 mm. Hold the loop about 50 mm away from the glasses, and wrap the leading end around the two strands of cord, two times, working downward. And on the third turn bring the leading end through the loop at the top, from behind. Holding the leading end firmly, push your newly made coils upward; this closes up the loop, and traps the leading end, so it won't come undone.

Then pull the coils back toward the frame by tugging on the long length of cord.

Do exactly the same on the other side.

Now we're moving onto slidey knots. These knots will adjust your necklace. We're using two different-colored cords to make it easier to understand, but once you've grasped the technique you can use any color you like.

We'll start at the blue end. Fold the blue end back 100 mm, then lay it parallel to the red cord, so that the two cut ends are next to each other.

Wrap the blue end around the blue and red cord three times. On the fourth, thread it through the loop at the top, from behind.

Next, push the coils upward, pulling on the long blue cord, until the blue cord is trapped. You'll know if you've done it right if the red cord moves freely through the knot. Be careful not to pull it right through, or all your knottiness will be undone.

We have a borderline obsession with finding things with ladies' faces on them.

Now we're heading for the red cord. Fold the red end back on itself by 100 mm, and wrap it around three times. On the fourth, thread it through the loop at the top, from behind.

Then push the coils upward, as before, pulling on the long red cord. Again, make sure it's good and tight.

You should now have two slidey knots.

Now get the superglue out.

On the knots next to the glasses, dab some superglue on the reverse of the knot, where the leading end is poking out. The glue secures the knot and it'll stop the cord fraying when you cut it. Let the glue dry.

When the glue's dry, go ahead and neatly snip, with the needlework scissors, the excess of the cord, so that you get a nice, neat, stubby knot.

On the slidey knots put a tiny touch of superglue on the loose ends close to the knots. DON'T glue the moving cord.

Let the glue dry, and snip off the excess.

A Final
Word

It's the end of our book, but, hopefully, the start of your adventure. You've got all the techniques in hand, now it's all about giving it a go.

It can be a bit scary to embark on your own, so enlist a few like-minded friends and head to your nearest thrift store or yard sale, collect some treasure and spend an afternoon creating some heading-out-on-the-town jewelry. Hopefully the book will have inspired you, but so will your friends. Sharing ideas, looking over each other's shoulders, experimenting, suggesting what looks good with what is all part of the fun—and you never know where it'll lead!

After we left college, we had a few ideas, a lot of enthusiasm and a great bunch of friends. We enlisted them when we had to make our first collection on that mad weekend twelve years ago, chatting in a sunny garden about all the things that we could make. And because we talked nonstop about Tatty Devine we made more friends who inspired us to try new things, or collaborated with us on some our favorite projects. At the Cast-Off knitting club, we dropped stitches, and at the Mangle studios we got bonkers images printed on belts and purses and met artist Rob Ryan, who makes the most romantic, intricate paper cuts. He wanted to make a piece of jewelry that described what was in his heart, and he made us think what was in our hearts, which was the loveliest thing to think about; we've worked with him ever since. And we jumped at the chance to work with the band Belle and Sebastian; their music has been the soundtrack to our lives, so making a Dog on Wheels brooch was like a dream come true.

When we started we would never have imagined that we'd have two shops, an online boutique, and that we'd be stocked in over 200 shops worldwide. One of our most popular pieces is the name necklace. We first made these as Christmas presents for all of the friends who helped us out; other people saw them and wondered where they could get them from, so we started making

them to sell. Now even Katy Perry has one. But we still love the same things that we've always loved—putting on art shows in the Brick Lane shop, buying records, Dumpster diving and making things. And there's nothing stopping you from doing the same sort of things—like putting on an exhibition in your bedroom or in a pop-up tent in the garden, making a piece of handmade jewelry as a birthday gift or designing a birthday card and getting busy with the glitter.

We know that nothing beats the satisfaction of getting the glue gun out or the drill and creating something genius.

We'd love to see what you've come up with! Send us pictures of your projects, tells us what inspires you and where you wore your latest, newly created piece of jewelry.

And it doesn't matter if it all goes wrong. Sometimes mistakes lead to the best inventions, but help is at hand if you want to try to rescue something or are stuck on a fiddly technique, head to our website for practical advice.

Inspiration is everywhere; all you need to do is go and look for it! So are you ready to begin exploring?

Here's our online address: www.tattydevine.com.

Crafty Shopping
with Tatty Devine

We've said it before and we'll say it again: "One girl's trash is another girl's treasure."

We are constantly visiting yard sales, thrift stores and flea markets, rummaging through old stuff, on the lookout for random junk that can be transformed into something cool. Check out the classifieds or your nearest yard sale, and be prepared to get up nice and early to get the best stuff. You could even go on a thrift store crawl. Canvass an area, get on a train, wear comfortable shoes, eat fries for lunch.

Index